Utterly Loved

Kat Bastion

Foreword *by Sylvain Reynard*

UTTERLY LOVED

UTTERLY LOVED

ISBN-13: 978-0615729206
ISBN-10: 0615729207

DEDICATION

This book is a love letter written to the love of my life, my husband.
My best friend. My confidant. My partner. My true north. My prince.
… My soul mate.

Our time together has been idyllic, passionate, surprising, and miraculous.
Through it all, we have held tightly to each other with the fiercest love I have
ever known.

I'm incredibly grateful for all our history. Every tear of joy and heartache.
Because of the amazing journey thus far, we live a better life.

With all my heart, I look forward to the rest of our lives.
…One amazing moment at a time.

UTTERLY LOVED

TABLE OF CONTENTS

	Acknowledgments	vii
	Foreword *by Sylvain Reynard*	ix
1	The Fall	3
2	Eternal Kiss	7
3	Unwritten Path	11
4	Dance With Me	17
5	Stolen Night	21
6	Lost Is Found With You	25
7	Blame It On The Moon	29
8	Trees Of Jasmine	33
9	Shelter Me	37
10	Beautiful Seasons	41
11	Utterly Loved	45
12	Heaven… Found	49
13	Blue Green	53
14	Sun In My Eyes	57
15	Undone	61
16	Awakening	65
17	Love Unfurled	69

18   Saturday Morning   73

19   Something About Snow   77

20   Sum of Days   81

21   Transcendence   85

     About The Author   89

ACKNOWLEDGMENTS

No amount of words could ever express my heartfelt appreciation for the depth of endless support and encouragement that I receive from my husband, for whom the idea for this collection of poetry was originally conceived. After all these years, you surprise me yet again with something I was completely unaware of… your love and knowledge of poetry.
Ever my guide in everything.

"Speshul" thanks go to PipPit. My daily cheerleader and fervent supporter. Your constant words of praise and encouragement are beyond uplifting. Thank you for sticking with me even on my craziest days.

Appreciation goes to Sylvain Reynard for both kindling a love for writing poetry that I had no idea existed within me, and for his humanitarian efforts, which lit before me a road paved with possibilities.

Thanks go to all of my Twitter friends and blog followers for the unexpected enthusiastic love of my poetic words. Were it not for your outpour of support, I likely would not have made this collection public.

Finally, and most importantly, I would like to thank every purchaser of this book. I decided to share my heartfelt words with the world to help others. So many people have never known what it is like to be loved in *any* form. My mission is to reach out and show them they are loved.

Utterly Loved is my first published work, and due to the unforeseen gift of my poetry and my deep-seated need to help others, not one dollar will ever line my pockets. Thank you for enjoying the poetry and joining the cause.

Please tell two friends about this book. Please tell twenty. Promote and encourage others to buy *Utterly Loved*, not only to directly benefit those who desperately need our love, but to bring awareness to the fact that so many are less fortunate than we are.

The question "Just because you can, should you?" should be answered with a resounding yes.

Be the difference…what you hold in your hands is a part of that difference.

How much difference can one person make?

{smiles slowly}

Dream big. I do.

FOREWORD

One need only look at the news in order to discover that our world is troubled. There are wars and armed conflicts, poverty and starvation, human trafficking and child exploitation. It's enough to make one want to turn off the news and think about something else.

Avoidance might be helpful as a short term coping mechanism, but it isn't going to change anything. Eventually, we have to be willing to confront the problems in our world. We need to be the change that we seek.

To combat poverty and injustice, we can become activists. We can protest local and federal governments. Certainly, it's worthwhile to fight for justice, both legal and social. But it's even more important to be just, to be kind, to be compassionate.

It's common for celebrities and politicians to champion various causes and to lend their names to fundraisers. It's less common for novelists to do so, although in my short foray into fiction writing I've come to know a number of writers who have done just that. Kat Bastion is one of them.

There's a tradition in many cultures of setting aside part of one's income or goods to give to the poor. In the modern world, many of us tend to give spontaneously to this homeless person, to this cause that we believe in, or to our local food bank. But the weakness of spontaneity is that it isn't consistent or long term, and charities rely on long-term donations and volunteers for sustainability. With this book of poetry, Kat is donating the proceeds to help those in need. She's setting aside her income, long term, in order to make a change, and she's chosen to support World Vision and Covenant House.

(continued)

Both World Vision and Covenant House are important to me. They have as their mission a commitment to helping the poor, especially children and young people, and providing a safe place for those in danger or crisis. They are the hands and feet and food and homes of donors, going to places donors cannot or will not go. They are our proxies. But they can only help others if we help them through our donations.

Thanks for being the change our world needs,

Sylvain Reynard

www.sylvainreynard.com

❧

I am truly blessed, for I am loved. My heart aches for all who
have never known love. May I brighten their world with hope.

❧

കൗങ

The Fall

Misted platinum wafting by lures a nymph to dance,

Sprinkles falling, laughter rising, spinning pure romance.

Fragile wings spiral higher, flirting with the sun.

Captured by a passerby, innocence begone.

Discarded leaves tumble past in muted reddish hues,

Coldness slowly settles in, vibrance does recuse.

Sadness looks with longing eyes out into the world,

Kindness brings a soft caress, silken wings unfurl.

Loving smile, a whispered touch, sends a soul to soar.

Bonds are broken in sweet flight, freedom evermore.

To the heavens angel flies, heartbeat starts to stall,

Grounded, solid arms do reach, there to catch the fall.

ॐ

ဆဘၓ

ॐ

Surrendering completely gifts absolute freedom.

ॐ

ജരൃ

Eternal Kiss

Anticipation quickens heated pulse,
Chaste shoulder massage evoked.

Bold hands brush soft hair aside,
Thoughts race, mind drifts, hazes.

Uncertain wonder, desire overcomes,
Slow inhalation, firm fingers graze,
Ribs, curve of breast, collarbone.

Subtle invitation offered, received,
Fall into welcome, coy smile flirting.
Dark eyes, words murmured in tease.

Reclining back, we tumble together,
Arms tangled in warm embrace.

Heartbeat thunders, left breathless,
Cheeks caressed, pure reverence.

Tender lips, barest touch promises,
Electric spark, gasps, amazement.

Awestruck moment treasured slowly,
Bonding scent savored completely,
Champagne bubbles dance sweetly.

Entire world pauses, suspended
Eternity… captured in a kiss.

৵৶

ജ⊗ൽ

❧

In the sleep-blurred edges of a slowly waking mind, inhale deeply, see the dark world, and decide the day will be good.

❧

ଅଚ୍ଚ

Unwritten Path

From afar draws closest friend
Warm smile lights across my face
Until innocence falters
My father's hand you embrace

One gentlemanly gesture
Caught unaware of feeling
On a gasp heart truly flipped
The unprepared sent reeling

Uncertainty ruled for days
Emotion possibly dreamed
Two continued platonic
No longer all that it seemed

Unsure steps had to happen
Small flirting cast in short line
Daring brushes of bodies
A quest of response in kind

Pulse raced like frightened rabbit
Fearing a one-sided crush
Cold night your jacket provided
Tighter hold sending a rush

Risk rewarded seduction
Boundaries blessedly crossed
Though bliss gifted brave-hearted
Hazard signs still marked the lost

(continued)

ঝ○৪

Grateful for every moment
Truth safe under lock and key
Partner willing when ready
Hesitant wait patiently

Walls crumble, trust building high
Relaxed unbridled laughter
Words spilled to speechless awestruck
Shock eased with loving banter

Strength had grown invincible
In power-charged aftermath
Finding joy ever after
Blazing our unwritten path

৩৩

‽ℭℬ

৵৶

Only when we take the leap, unafraid to fall, do we learn to fly.

৵৶

ૹჯდ

Dance With Me

Your outstretched hand
A soft knowing smirk
Undeniable invitation

Bodies pull close
Desiring eyes connect
Indescribable fascination

Hitched breath, a gasp
Fiercely captured kiss
Unbelievable revelation

Strong arms in lead
Willing heart follows
Inescapable destination

Music ending
Fresh air enchanting
Unavoidable deviation

Dance continues
Slow private tango
Irresistible provocation

ഇ൞

ಬಒಃ

❧

When the storm rages, be the beacon.

❧

ဆာ၆ဒ

Stolen Night

Fingers lace, random course charted,
Forest shimmers in butterflies.
Colors flash hot iridescence,
Kaleidoscope tempts widened eyes.

Untamed river leads brave ones through,
Shadowed tunnel carved in limestone.
Antics cause free-flowing laughter,
Wet kisses, cavern made our own.

Chase falling sun to catch the sights,
Rainbow birds fly in tropic breeze.
Spicy flavors make mouths water,
Paradise, due north of Belize.

Twilight drops in gray-shrouding cloak,
Scouting finds columns of mushrooms.
Last stumble as light fades away,
Secret room decked in orchid blooms.

Abandoned park, left far behind,
Tribal drums set our hearts on fire.
Gifted fortune for wild romance,
Both shark and turtle fin inspire.

Pathway swathed in inky darkness,
Meanders to deserted cove.
Toes buried in white sugared sand,
Palm tree and hammock treasure trove.

Full moon guards glittering black sea,
Horizon, ship in sparkling lights.
Two began a day's adventure,
Excited lovers stole the night.

❧

৪৩৫৪

ॐ

With a hopeful heart, stretch out your arms and welcome the sun. You invite the radiant warmth that brightens your world.

ॐ

ഠഗ

Lost Is Found With You

Against the grain we fly due north,
…excited
Pavement left for path uncharted.

Sounds hush as ancient pines embrace,
…fascinate
Waist-high fields in gold undulate.

Shadowed aspen gift spirals down,
…fluttering
Sprite opens brightly painted wing.

Wrong turn transforms into fortune,
…completely
Nature traps us in reverie.

Promised safety in arms wrapped tight,
…absolute
Adventure winds past fern and newt.

Blue skies capture two that wandered,
…overdue
Without a doubt, lost is found with you.

ॐॐ

ഇരൽ

꙾

Kiss me. Capture my lips like you're starving for air…
and I'm your last breath of oxygen.

꙾

෨Ӂൠ

Blame It On The Moon

Black velvet sky ablaze with stars,

Truly blooms the love of ours.

A smile lights up a stolen glance,

Lovers blessed to have the chance.

Snowy egrets take to flight,

The pair on wing into the night.

We dash away to take our time,

A feathered touch, so sublime.

Thermal currents make me soar,

Waves crash down upon the shore.

I hold you close, floating high,

From every gasp and trembled sigh.

When sleep claims us way too soon…

      … I blame it on the moon.

க௸

ହୠଓଷ

❧

Loved. Totally. Completely. Unequivocally. Loved.

❧

80〇〇3

Trees of Jasmine

Young lovers walking hand in hand,

Teased and laughed along cobblestone track.

They walked among trees of jasmine,

And spoke of a place called Tamarack.

Church mice happy to have a crumb,

Feasted at balls like faraway kings,

But at their cozy home and hearth,

The two alone cherished finer things.

Escape to a path few had tread,

Brought flowers by a rushing stream.

Curving trail… you lead, I follow.

In your loving arms is where I dream.

❦

ଔଔଔ

∾

Breaking waves wash ashore new beginnings.

∾

ജാബ

Shelter Me

I am darkness

You are light

Shelter me into the night

I was lost

Love was found

Walk with me on sacred ground

Warmth of day

Shining bright

Protective arms hold me tight

Softest kiss

Sweetest sound

Two as one forever bound

ക

ഉന്ദ

ऊ∽๑

Eyes lit with hope could power the world.

ॐ∽ల

೮೦Ж೮ಽ

Beautiful Seasons

Spring's fragile flower
Promise to protect
From harsh rain shower
Or drought of neglect

Summer's strong oak tree
Will cherish and love
Chitter of squirrels
Peace of nesting dove

Fall's bright autumn moon
Shines praise in honor
Gleaming true guide light
Sweet slumber under

Winter's crystal frost
Claims a special hold
Treasure for new life
Stories to unfold

Beautiful seasons
Unique in blessing
Entwine united
Graced in their wedding

❧

ೞೞಐ

❧

When silence becomes a heartbeat, the world flows in with music.

❧

৪৩০৪

Utterly Loved

Accepting me as I am, stripped bare
Each facet honored in tender care

Kindness lifts high like a miracle
Weakness transformed to invincible

Shone beautiful from the inside out
Beamed brightly in daylight rooftop shout

Truly cherished I've been made to feel
Aching emotion, heart bursts surreal

Words rendered wholly inadequate
The closest any come to describe it

  … Utterly Loved

❧

ဆဌ

❧

The light that saves us is the spark inside… kindled with the slightest breath of hope.

❧

☙✄ও

Heaven... Found

I settle into the moment.

Time stalls.

The world... falls away.

I nestle closer.

Lips... nuzzle.

Pulse... thrums.

Musky scent... intoxicating.

Salty taste... captivating.

Strong arms embrace.

I sigh.

Warmth spreads.

Silence reigns.

A moment... forever captured.

Safe.

Protected.

Loved.

I am... unbound.

Heaven... found.

ৡঌ

ଔଓଔଓ

ജ交

Unleash passion from your heart like rolling thunder.

ഇ交

೮ Youಣ

Blue Green

Milestone marked by getaway lost
Smooth-shifting gears lock way down low
Taste of sweet guava-mango nectar
Salty mist cools as breezes blow

Bright eyes soak up stunning island
Colorscape lush in blue and green
Glittering jewels sashay on cue
Brilliant dance in crystal marine

Grass-thatched bure over glass floor
Kids turned upside-down on the bed
Tart of the day tempts our palates
Unplugged from life, recharge instead

Beachcombers liberate their fun
Voyage in a kayak for two
Aquatic life thrives beneath us
Before great Mt. Otemanu

Fly in lagoon with sea angels
Walk on deck ushered by blacktip
Serene dinner by candlelight
Cozy desserts highlight the trip

Sun sets over glorious scene
Waves ebb along white coral shore
Hearts burst abundant love and joy
  … paradise evermore

෨෬

଼ଓଔ

❧

A selfless gesture… Life's greatest treasure.

❧

છેપ્ર

Sun In My Eyes

Forest of secrets
Haven to all
Darkest days find
Gray-misted shawl

Tender gift's promise
Protected by thorn
Shelter granted
Fierce storm reborn

Regardless of cold
Deep velvet night
Falls silent hush
Patient for light

Bright hope in glimmers
Song greets the dawn
Trembling yearning
Solace grows strong

In radiant embrace
Joyous heart cries
Your stunning love
The sun in my eyes

so-co

ഐൽൽ

༸

Seduce the mind... The heart will follow.

༺

ಬಂಗ

Undone

Storm building
Heat rising
Darted glance
You feel the same

Heart racing
Breath panting
Stolen chance
I throw the game

Deep aching
Eyes pleading
No mercy
You're in the lead

Slow touching
Warm rushing
So sultry
I'm lost in need

Lips gasping
Back arching
Your body
Pulls mine undone

Cries rasping
Waves crashing
My body
With yours as one

৵৹৶

ෆ006ෂ

❧

Go forth. Share your smile. Ignite hope in another.

❧

಼ೲೞ

Awakening

Reclining on abandoned beach
Exhaling worldly cares away
Slow waves wash through open minds
New perspective's potent ballet

Breezes cast aloft complex webs
Contented eyes bid bon voyage
Sunset bursts deep painted colors
Awakening's brilliant homage

Darkened vastness crisps in focus
A billion pinpoints glittering
Souls see everything possible
Hearts dream while raptly listening

Ideas soar on untamed winds
Adventure rides kinetic flow
Two hands entwine as smiles abound
Secrets breathed, righteous set aglow

Gifts of wonder greet the ready
Life's most amazing accident
Dawn breaks resplendent hopeful day
Gleaming treasure shared abundant

❧

శుల్జ

❧

My mind unravels,
thoughts flowing into the wind like purest spun gold.

❧

ৰাঞ্চ

Love Unfurled

Heart is found where connected
Love blooms forth least expected

Round eyes stare in hopefulness
Grace shines warmth in soft caress

Hero grants a selfless gift
Lost no longer left adrift

Saved beam bright adoring smiles
Warriors fight across the miles

Kindness spreads with love unfurled
Peace ignites around the world

ച

ଯୁଓଔ

ॐ

Share love. One thing in our harsh world that costs nothing...
Worth everything.

ॐ

ഇൗൟ

Saturday Morning

Silence reigns as dawn approaches
Darkest room banishes twilight
Stretching out, blissful warmth is sought
Treasure found as embrace wraps tight

Hot breath teases a bare shoulder
Strong heartbeat coaxes happy sighs
Limbs tangle, claiming possession
Nuzzled neck, soft purr with closed eyes

Deep breathing, tender caressing
Slow and easy, no plans in sight
Knowing bodies start exploring
Love's surrender, pleasure so right

Demands do require an answer
Heart and soul can utter no lies
For if it's Saturday morning
They'll get our favorite alibis

&

ಜಿಡ

⤞⤝

In your arms, I sigh in comfort; inhale, absorbing peace; and radiate the love and hope I've found sharing it with the world.

⤝⤞

಄಄

Something About Snow

In delicate whispers it falls
Near rainbow-twisted icicles

Parachutes drift in patterned lace
Branches frosted with tender grace

Sparkling clear diamond days arrive
Foot-printed forest brought to life

Swooshing turns on fallen powder
Playground starts contagious laughter

Steaming hot tub, beautiful view
Perfect snowman molded by two

Through window fogged by warming fire
Snow beckons forth sweetest desire

৵৶

೮೦೮೪

෨ංෆ

Humbly accept love. Treasure the gift as warmth glows within.
Inhale sweet peace until bliss bursts forth, embracing another.

ఞంౡ

ଚ୬ଙ୍ଗ

Sum of Days

Children play at spring's picnic
Hand of fate cast romantic

Pair do meet once decades pass
Shifted sands in hourglass

Kids again, joyous wonder
Mountain peaks, rolling thunder

Sage advice from late hour talks
Trust is forged in miles of walks

Sparks fire flame astonishing
Lighting fuse, two entangling

Best of friends become lovers
Deepened bond under covers

Hearts collide in true soul mate
Seamless halves appreciate

Promise made, reverent vow
Future told from here and now

Perfect bodies loved so much
Starving lips yet softest touch

Vessels safe-keep what is dear
Heart and soul for holding near

When our sum of days grow long
On front porch with silent song

Pure love flows in peaceful right
Endlessly into the night

৵৵

ဆုသ

❧

In the darkest hour, the smallest act of kindness becomes the foundation of many miracles.

❧

ഇൽൽ

Transcendence

Breeze lifts tortoiseshell butterfly
Landing on purple petals soft
Rustling overhead branches bow
Errant gust casts ripe seed aloft

Fanned soil blankets in tender care
Spring witnesses burgeoning life
Winds ripple quivering sapling
Grown stronger from external strife

Regal tree touches brilliant sky
Snow flurry marks final season
Grandeur beside a Christmas hearth
Ribbons gleam in festive reason

Perfect night snuggled together
Blizzard curls around shaping drifts
Snowflakes frost glossy windowpane
Creaking heard as weathervane shifts

Voiced wonder if the story ends
Noble fir cut, holiday trimmed
Lips fall hushed with tenderest kiss
Never, my love… we are the wind

❧

ജാഗ

প৵

Leave the past behind, let the future guide, but make what you do in this moment matter.

ৡ৵

৪৩৫৩

ABOUT THE AUTHOR

Kat Bastion is an award-winning paranormal romance writer who stumbled into the charitable project of *Utterly Loved* quite accidentally. She wouldn't have it any other way, as some of the very best things in life are beautifully and perfectly serendipitous.

If you're curious about some of her epiphanies…

Over a year ago, a journey of self-discovery began with the goal of becoming a more selfless creature in the process.

In September of 2012, a wonderful family of friends on Twitter shared a love of Sylvain Reynard, who shared the poetry of Robert Frost, and inspiration ignited.

Kat's first poem, the second…third…were all memories, treasured moments. The idea for *Utterly Loved* was born… as a private twentieth anniversary gift to her love. Twenty poems for twenty years, plus one for the future.

Humanitarianism flowed hot and fast through her veins, support of her poetry rang loud and enthusiastically in commentary, and blessings of love burst from her heart and soul. The perfect storm coalesced into a burning need to share a poetic gift she never anticipated with the world.

There was never any question in Kat's mind. Every dollar, after costs and taxes, will go directly to charities helping the least fortunate in this world. They will feel *Utterly Loved.*

For a list of charities benefiting from the sales of *Utterly Loved*, please visit Kat Bastion's website at www.katbastion.com or her weekly blog at www.talktotheshoe.com and click on the tab or link entitled *Utterly Loved.*